BILIN

MW01609539

English-French vol. 2

by
Tracy Ayotte-Irwin
Music by Sara Jordan

Produced and Published by
Sara Jordan Publishing
a division of ℗©2003 Jordan Music Productions Inc.
(SOCAN)

ISBN 1 - 894262 - 78 - 6

Acknowledgments

Lyricist - Tracy Ayotte-Irwin

Editor - Marjelaine Caya

Composer and Producer - Sara Jordan

Music Coproducer, Arranger, Engineer - Mark Shannon

Male Singer - Peter Lebuis

Female Singer - Julie Crochetière

Digital Illustration Assistant - Ihab El-Shinnawy

Cover Design and Layout - Campbell Creative Services

Digitally Recorded and Mixed by Mark Shannon,
The TreeFort, Toronto, Ontario, 2003.

For further information contact:

Jordan Music Productions Inc.
M.P.O. Box 490
Niagara Falls, NY
U.S.A. 14302-0490

Jordan Music Productions Inc.
Station M, Box 160
Toronto, Ontario
Canada, M6S 4T3

Internet: http://www.sara-jordan.com
e-mail: sjordan@sara-jordan.com
Telephone: (800) 567-7733

To Anna and Brayden, with love.

À Anna et Brayden, avec amour.

We acknowledge the financial support of the Government of Canada through the Book Publishing Industry Development Program (BPIDP) for our publishing activities.

We acknowledge the Government of Ontario through the Ontario Media Development Corporation's Ontario Book Initiative.

Contents / Table des matières

Hints for Teachers

and Parents

As both a teacher and parent dealing with young people every day, I know how hard it is sometimes to pump excitement and interest into daily classes.

Second language learning research has shown that the use of the first language can aid and enhance the learning of a new language.

The intent of *Bilingual Songs, English-French, vol. 2*, is to liven up second language learning through the rhythm, melodies and exercises here which include *both* languages.

Second languages need not be strictly used during a certain block of time at school, but can be carried over into many other areas of study (be it music class, gym, drama or creative writing) and, most importantly, go beyond the classroom and become part of students' lives at home and in the community.

Sincerely,

Sara Jordan

President

A few ways to use this resource:

In the classroom:

- ☑ Songs 1 through 9 of this volume can be used to teach either French or English. Songs 10 through 12 concentrate on French grammar problems.
- ☑ Try lowering the volume of the language being taught to insure active student participation.
- ☑ This resource works well in independent learning resource centers as both a remedial tutorial and as an enriching exercise for advanced students who can write new lyrics using the music accompaniment tracks.
- ☑ As part of a Drama class, have the students act out the various songs. Great fun for "air-band" shows.
- ☑ Encourage students to cover some of the words of their second language (in the book) preferably vocabulary items or the verbs in the last songs and try to write them after hearing the song and with the help of their first language.

At home:

- ☑ Whether you listen on the family stereo, through a stereo headset, or in the car as you run errands, *Bilingual Songs, vol. 2* can be great fun and entertainment for the entire family.
- ☑ Try singing along using the lyrics book. Maybe you'll discover a star in your own home!

Introduction
Introduction

Hello! Good day to you!
We've new songs to sing for you.
There are lots of things to do
with 'Bilingual Songs, volume 2'.

Bonjour! Comment allez-vous?
Voici des chants nouveaux pour vous.
Des choses à faire, il y en a beaucoup
avec «Bilingual Songs, volume 2».

instrumental :

Let's sing in English and in French.
We will have a great time too.
It can be such fun to learn
with 'Bilingual Songs, volume 2'.

Chantons en anglais et en français,
nous nous amuserons beaucoup.
Que c'est donc plaisant d'apprendre
avec «Bilingual Songs, volume 2».

Counting to 30
Compter jusqu'à 30

chorus/*refrain* :

Have you seen the rabbits
that live in my backyard?

Every time I look outside
it seems that they have multiplied.
I try to count them but they hide
in my backyard.

> *Avez-vous vu les lapins*
> *qui vivent dans ma cour?*
>
> *Chaque fois que je regarde dehors,*
> *ils semblent se multiplier*
> *et quand j'essaie de les compter*
> *ils vont se cacher.*

Let's count together!
Comptons ensemble!

One, two, three,
Un, deux, trois,
four, five, six,
quatre, cinq, six,
seven, eight, nine,
sept, huit, neuf,
ten!
dix!

chorus/*refrain* :

Let's keep counting!
Continuons de compter!

Eleven, twelve, thirteen,
Onze, douze, treize,
fourteen, fifteen, sixteen,
quatorze, quinze, seize,

seventeen, eighteen, nineteen,
dix-sept, dix-huit, dix-neuf,
twenty!
vingt!

chorus/*refrain* :

Oh, no! I see some more!
Ah non! J'en vois d'autres!

Twenty-one, twenty-two, twenty-three,
Vingt et un, vingt-deux, vingt-trois,
twenty-four, twenty-five, twenty-six,
vingt-quatre, vingt-cinq, vingt-six,
twenty-seven, twenty-eight, twenty-nine,
vingt-sept, vingt-huit, vingt-neuf,
thirty!
trente!

chorus/*refrain* :

N° 3

Counting by Tens
Compter par dix

sing/*chantez* 2x :

I can count by tens.
> *Je peux compter par dix.*

You can count.
> *Tu peux compter.*

We can count by tens.

I can count by tens.
> *Je peux compter par dix.*

You can count.
> *Tu peux compter.*
> *Nous pouvons compter par dix.*

Ten, twenty,
thirty, forty, fifty,
sixty, seventy,
eighty, ninety and one hundred.

> *Dix, vingt,*
> *trente, quarante, cinquante,*
> *soixante, soixante-dix,*
> *quatre-vingts, quatre-vingt-dix et cent.*

Exercise / Exercice

Write the numbers.

Écrivez les nombres.

10   _____

20   _____

30   _____

40   _____

50   _____

60   _____

70   _____

80   _____

90   _____

100   _____

Shapes and Sizes
Les formes et les grandeurs

chorus/*refrain (2x)* :

Circles, squares and triangles;
many shapes and many angles.

Les cercles, les carrés et les triangles ;
beaucoup de formes et beaucoup d'angles.

Shapes come in different sizes:
wide or narrow, big or small,
long or short, thick or thin.
Do you know your shapes at all?

Les formes ont différentes grandeurs :
larges ou étroites, grandes ou petites,
longues ou courtes, épaisses ou minces.
Connaissez-vous vos formes aujourd'hui?

I can draw a circle
like a cinnamon apple pie.
I can draw a circle
like a full moon in the sky.

*Je peux faire un cercle
comme une tarte aux
      pommes et cannelle.
Je peux faire un cercle
comme une pleine lune dans le ciel.*

chorus/*refrain* :

Triangles have three sides
just like Christmas trees.
Triangles have three sides.
We can count them easily.

*Les triangles ont trois côtés
comme les sapins de Noël
      décorés.
Les triangles ont trois côtés.
Ils sont faciles à compter.*

Squares seem very perfect,
equal sides and angles.
Make a square or rectangle.
All you need are two triangles.

Les carrés semblent parfaits,
les côtés et les angles égaux.
Faites un rectangle ou un carré.
Deux triangles sont tout ce qu'il vous faut.

chorus/*refrain* :

Exercise / Exercice

Color the squares green.
Coloriez les carrés en vert.

Color the circles yellow.
Coloriez les cercles en jaune.

Color the rectangles blue.
Coloriez les rectangles en bleu.

Color the triangles red.
Coloriez les triangles en rouge.

We recommend you photocopy this page before coloring so as not to destroy the master book.

Nous vous recommendons de photocopier la page avant de colorier pour ne pas endommager votre cahier.

Emotions
Les émotions

chorus/*refrain :*

How is it that you're feeling?
How are you feeling today?
Are you optimistic
that things will go your way?

Or are you feeling tired and blue?
Do you feel like crying too?
Try to smile a little bit,
you'll see that it's good for you.

Comment te sens-tu, cher ami?
Comment te sens-tu aujourd'hui?
Es-tu optimiste?
Penses-tu que ta journée portera fruits?

Ou es-tu triste et fatigué?
As-tu envie de pleurer?
Essaie de sourire un peu
car c'est bon pour la santé.

Today, I am happy.
Aujourd'hui, je suis heureuse.

Today, I am sad.
Aujourd'hui, je suis triste.

Today, I am angry.
Aujourd'hui, je suis fâchée.

Today, I am confused.
Aujourd'hui, je suis confus.

chorus/*refrain* :

Today, I am frightened.
Aujourd'hui, j'ai peur.

Today, I am anxious.
Aujourd'hui, je suis anxieux.

Today, I am bored.
Aujourd'hui, je m'ennuie.

Today, I am surprised.
Aujourd'hui, je suis surpris.

chorus/*refrain* :

Exercise / Exercice

How are you feeling today?

Comment vous sentez-vous aujourd'hui?

_____

_____

_____

_____

How are you feeling today?

Comment vous sentez-vous aujourd'hui?

_____   _____

_____   _____

We recommend you photocopy this page before coloring so as not to destroy the master book.

Nous vous recommendons de photocopier la page avant de colorier pour ne pas endommager votre cahier.

The Countryside
La campagne

chorus/*refrain 2x :*

Let's take our bikes
on a very long ride.
We'll ride and explore
in the countryside.

> *Allons en vélo*
> *faire une longue promenade.*
> *Nous irons explorer*
> *le beau paysage.*

We'll see lakes and ponds.
> *Nous verrons des lacs et des étangs.*

We'll see rivers and streams.
> *Nous verrons des rivières et des ruisseaux.*

We'll see fields of wheat.
Nous verrons des champs de blé.

We'll see flowers and trees.
Nous verrons des fleurs et des arbres.

instrumental :

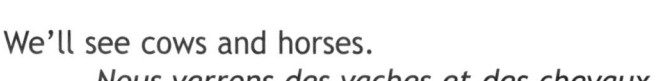

We'll see cows and horses.
Nous verrons des vaches et des chevaux.

We'll see chickens and goats.
Nous verrons des poules et des chèvres.

We'll see beautiful butterflies.
Nous verrons de beaux papillons.

We'll see insects and birds.
Nous verrons des insectes et des oiseaux.

chorus/*refrain* :

Our Community
Notre communauté

chorus/*refain* :

Let's go for a walk
around the town.
We'll see the important spots
around the town.

> *Allons nous promener*
> *partout en ville.*
> *Nous visiterons les lieux importants*
> *partout en ville.*

The doctor, the dentist,
the grocery store,
the big train station.
Wait! There's more.

> *Le médecin, le dentiste*
> *le supermarché,*
> *la gare de train.*
> *Attend, il en reste à explorer!*

chorus/*refrain* :

The bus, the bookstore
and the bakery,
the community center,
for my friends and me.

L'autobus, la librairie
et la boulangerie,
le centre communautaire,
pour moi et mes amis.

chorus/*refrain* :

Opposites
Les contraires

chorus/*refrain* :

Let's sing about things that oppose.
I say open, you say close.
I say first, you say last.
I say future, you say past.

> *Chantons à propos des contraires.*
> *Je dis ouvert, tu dis fermé.*
> *Je dis premier, tu dis dernier.*
> *Je dis l'avenir, tu dis le passé.*

Spoken part:

The opposite of tall is short.
> *Le contraire de grand est petit.*
The opposite of fat is thin.
> *Le contraire de gros est mince.*

The opposite of empty is full.
Le contraire de vide est plein.
The opposite of heavy is light.
Le contraire de lourd est léger.

chorus/*refrain* :

The opposite of tomorrow is yesterday.
Le contraire de demain est hier.
The opposite of day is night.
Le contraire du jour est la nuit.

The opposite of backward is forward.
Le contraire de reculer est avancer.
The opposite of up is down.
Le contraire d'en haut est en bas.

chorus/*refrain* :

Measurement
Les mesures

chorus/*refrain* :

Hi!
I'm the Measuring Man.
I measure everything that I can.
Temperature, weight,
        amount and time;
my computations work out fine!

Salut!
Je suis l'expert des mesures.
Je mesure tout ce que je peux :
la température, le poids,
la quantité et le temps.
Mes calculs fonctionnent tout le temps.

Rulers and tape measures,
measure length and width.
How tall are you?
I am 5 feet tall. (1.5 metres)

*Les règles servent à mesurer
la longueur et la largeur.
Quelle est ta grandeur?
Je mesure cinq pieds. (1,5 mètres)*

chorus (English) :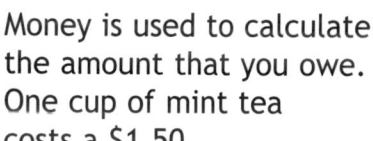

Clocks and watches
are used to measure time.
What time is it?
It is 9 o'clock.

*Les horloges et les montres
nous indiquent l'heure.
Quelle heure est-il?
Il est 9 heures.*

refrain (en français) :

Money is used to calculate
the amount that you owe.
One cup of mint tea
costs a $1.50.

*L'argent sert à calculer
la somme que vous devez.
Une tasse de tisane à la menthe
coûte 1,50 $.*

chorus (English) :

People use scales
to measure weight.
How much do you weigh?
I am 122 pounds. (55 kg)

On utilise une balance
pour connaître le poids.
Combien pèses-tu?
Je pèse 122 livres. (55 kg)

refrain (en français) :

Exercises / Exercices

Measurement and Opposites

Les mesures et les contraires

The measuring cup is _____.

La tasse à mesurer est _____.

The measuring cup is _____.

La tasse à mesurer est _____.

We recommend you photocopy this page before coloring so as not to destroy the master book.

Nous vous recommendons de photocopier la page avant de colorier pour ne pas endommager votre cahier.

Exercises / Exercices

Measurement and Opposites

Les mesures et les contraires

The man is _____.

Cet homme est _____.

The man is _____.

Cet homme est _____.

We recommend you photocopy this page before coloring so as not to destroy the master book.

Nous vous recommendons de photocopier la page avant de colorier pour ne pas endommager votre cahier.

'To Be' and 'To Have'
«Avoir» et «être»

chorus/*refrain* :

'To have' and **'to be'**
are important verbs they say.
We need to know them well because
we use them every day!

Les verbes «avoir» et «être»
sont des verbes très importants.
Il faut bien les connaître
car on s'en sert très souvent.

We'll conjugate the verbs together.
Practice, it will take
to use the verbs **'avoir'** and **'être'**
without making mistakes.

Nous allons conjuguer ensemble
pour bien se pratiquer
à utiliser les verbes «avoir» et «être»
sans jamais se tromper.

Let's start with the verb **'avoir'**
which means 'to have' in French.

I have	*J'ai*
You have	*Tu as*
He has	*Il a*
She has	*Elle a*
We have	*Nous avons*
You have	*Vous avez*
They have	*Ils ou elles ont*

Now, let's practice the verb **'être'**
which means 'to be' in French.

I am	*Je suis*
You are	*Tu es*
He is	*Il est*
She is	*Elle est*
We are	*Nous sommes*
You are	*Vous êtes*
They are	*Ils ou elles sont*

chorus/*refrain* :

'To have' and **'to be'**
are important verbs they say.
We need to know them well because
we use them every day!

*Les verbes «**avoir**» et «**être**»*
sont des verbes très importants.
Il faut bien les connaître
car on s'en sert très souvent.

Exercises / Exercices

Exercises Using '*Être*'

Fill in the blanks with the verb '*être*'.
Remplissez les espaces avec le verbe «être».

Il _____ un garçon.

Elles _____ tristes.

Nous _____ contents.

Je _____ ton médecin.

Vous _____ mes cousins.

Je _____ nerveux.

Jean et Claude _____ au zoo ensemble.

Lisa _____ anglaise.

Jean _____ au centre communautaire.

Exercises / Exercices

Exercises Using 'Avoir'

Fill in the blanks with the verb 'avoir'.
Remplissez les espaces avec le verbe «avoir».

J' _____ un chien.

Tu _____ plusieurs amis.

Ils _____ des bonbons.

Elle _____ une jupe rouge.

Nous _____ des chevaux.

Sophie _____ 12 ans.

Vous _____ froid.

Nous _____ du café.

Il _____ une règle.

'Avoir' for 'To Be'

Quand «to be» devient «avoir»

chorus/refrain 2x :

We must be careful
not to make mistakes
by sometimes saying 'je suis'
when we should say 'j'ai'.

> On doit faire attention
> de ne pas se tromper.
> On dit parfois «je suis»
> lorsqu'on devrait dire «j'ai».

When one translates from English
'I am' becomes 'je suis'.
But be careful because sometimes
that's not how it should be.

> Lorsqu'on traduit de l'anglais
> «I am» devient «je suis».
> Mais faites bien attention car parfois
> ce n'est pas ainsi!

Listen closely
to the following examples
you will see when
'I am' becomes 'j'ai'.

I am hungry.	*J'ai faim.*
I am thirsty.	*J'ai soif.*
I am cold.	*J'ai froid.*
I am hot.	*J'ai chaud.*

*Écoutez attentivement
les exemples suivants.
Vous verrez quand
«I am» devient «j'ai».*

I am twelve.	*J'ai douze ans.*
I am scared.	*J'ai peur.*
I am ashamed.	*J'ai honte.*
I am finished.	*J'ai fini.*

chorus/*refrain 2x* :

We must be careful
not to make mistakes
by sometimes saying *'je suis'*
when we should say *'j'ai'*.

> *On doit faire attention*
> *de ne pas se tromper.*
> *On dit parfois «je suis»*
> *lorsqu'on devrait dire «j'ai».*

When one translates from English
'I am' becomes *'je suis'*.
But be careful because sometimes
that's not how it should be.

> *Lorsqu'on traduit de l'anglais*
> *«I am» devient «je suis».*
> *Mais faites bien attention car parfois*
> *ce n'est pas ainsi!*

Nº 12

Connaître and/et savoir

chorus/*refrain* :

'**Connaître**' and '**savoir**'
are both used when saying '**to know**'.
You have to choose the right verb,
as this little song shows.

> «**Connaître**» et «**savoir**»
> *sont faciles à mêler.*
> *Pour bien choisir le verbe*
> *il faut bien y penser.*

To indicate knowing someone,
use the verb '**connaître**'
as in "I know John and Marie."
"You know Sophie."

> *Pour parler de quelqu'un*
> *on utilise le verbe* «**connaître**».
> «*Je **connais** Jean et Marie.*»
> «*Tu **connais** Sophie.*»

instrumental:

When referring to a place,
like a city or a country,
use *'connaître'* in these cases
as in "We know Italy."

Pour parler d'un endroit
comme une ville ou un pays,
on utilise le verbe «connaître».
«Nous connaissons l'Italie.»

chorus/*refrain* :

If you know a fact
and you know that it is true
'savoir' is the verb to use
like "I know what to do."

Si on sait un fait
et on sait que c'est vrai,
on utilise le verbe «savoir».
«Je sais ce que je fais.»

instrumental :

To indicate an ability,
a skill that you can do
use the verb '*savoir*'
as in "He knows how to cook."

Lorsqu'on parle d'une habileté,
quelque chose que nous faisons,
on utilise le verbe «savoir».
«Il sait faire la cuisson.»

chorus/*refrain* :

Exercises / Exercices

'*Avoir*' versus '*Être*'

Describe this boy in 3 sentences by correctly using examples for the verbs '*avoir*' and '*être*' from song 11.

Décrivez ce garçon en 3 phrases en suivant correctement les exemples des verbes «avoir» et «être» de la chanson 11.

Exercises / Exercices

Choosing 'connaître' or 'savoir'

Circle the right verb.
Encerclez le verbe approprié.

Je (sais ou connais) votre numéro de téléphone.

Vous (savez ou connaissez) ma mère?

Elle (sait ou connaît) la ville de Toronto.

Je ne (sais ou connais) pas cette personne.

Il (sait ou connaît) comment mesurer des maisons.

Tout le monde (sait ou connaît) qu'il y a des animaux au zoo.

Je (sais ou connais) les mois de l'année.

Vous (savez ou connaissez) quel temps il fait?

Ils (savent ou connaissent) tous les élèves de cette classe.

Elles (savent ou connaissent) compter par dix.

Tu (sais ou connais) bien mon oncle Gabriel?

Ask your retailer about other excellent audio programs by teacher Sara Jordan

Songs and Activities for Early Learners™

Dynamic songs teach the alphabet, counting, parts of the body, members of the family, colors, shapes, fruit and more. Helps students of all ages to learn basic vocabulary easily. The kit includes a lyrics book with activities teachers may reproduce for their classes.
IN ENGLISH, FRENCH OR SPANISH

Thematic Songs for Learning Language™

Delightful collection of songs and activities teaching salutations, rooms of the house, pets, meals, food and cutlery, transportation, communication, parts of the body, clothing, weather and prepositions. (Great for ESL classes.) The kit includes a lyrics book with activities teachers may reproduce for their classes.
IN ENGLISH, FRENCH OR SPANISH

Funky Phonics® and more...vol. 1

Reading Readiness comes with a lyrics book which includes helpful hints for parents and teachers. This great introduction to reading uses both phonics and whole language approaches. Topics covered include the alphabet, vowels, consonants, telling time, days of the week, seasons, the environment and more!!
IN ENGLISH, FRENCH OR SPANISH

Grammar Grooves vol.1™

Ten songs that teach about nouns, pronouns, adjectives, verbs, tenses, adverbs and punctuation. Activities and puzzles, which may be reproduced, are included in the lyrics book to help reinforce learning even further. A complement of music tracks to the 10 songs is included for karaoke performances. Also great for music night productions.
IN ENGLISH, FRENCH OR SPANISH

The Conjugation Series

Entertaining songs teach conjugations of high frequency verbs in the present, past and future tenses including irregular verbs. The accompanying lyrics/activity book includes exercises that can be reproduced by the classroom teacher.
IN FRENCH OR SPANISH

The 3R Rap®

Teaches multiplication from 2 to 12 with cross-curricular topics such as computers, noise pollution, etc. Side B includes music only tracks for student performances and/or creative writing assignments. Good as upgrading resource for older students. IN ENGLISH OR FRENCH.

Lullabies Around the World

*** Parents' Choice Award Winner! ***

Traditional lullabies sung by native singers with translated verses in English. Multicultural activities are included in the lyrics book. Includes a complement of music tracks for class performances. Pre-K - Grade 3   11 DIFFERENT LANGUAGES

Healthy Habits™

*** Directors' Choice Award Winner! ***

Songs and activities for Pre-K to Grade 3 covering nutrition, the food pyramid, anatomy, dental hygiene, personal and fire safety. The lyrics book which accompanies the recording has activities which can be reproduced for a class. A complement of music-only tracks works well for performances. IN ENGLISH

The Presidents' Rap®

from Washington to George W. Bush. The legends of the American Presidents live on in classical, swing, dixie, pop and rap music.A musical treasure trove of tid-bits of information on each President. Very popular among teachers wanting to put on musical shows in their school. IN ENGLISH

The Math Unplugged™ Series

Available for Addition, Subtraction, Division and Multiplication. Tuneful songs teach kids the basic math facts. Repetitive, musical and fun. A great resource. Each audio kit includes a lyrics book with worksheet pages that may be reproduced. IN ENGLISH

Celebrate the Human Race™

*** Directors' Choice Award Winner! ***
Learn about The Seven Natural Wonders of the world and the children who live in those places. Music is representative of each country or place studied. The kit includes a lyrics book with activities teachers may reproduce for their classes. IN ENGLISH

Celebrate Seasons™

A delightful collection of songs and activities about fall and deciduous trees, migration and hibernation, how animals prepare for winter, spring and maple syrup, flowers and pollination, solstices and equinoxes and how seasons differ in other parts of the world. The lyrics book includes related activities which teachers are free to reproduce for classroom use. A complement of instrumental versions of the ten songs makes class performances a breeze! IN ENGLISH

Celebrate Holidays™

An inspiring collection of songs and activities teaching about Halloween, Thanksgiving, Chanukah, Christmas, New Year's Celebrations, Valentine's Day, St. Patrick's Day and Easter plus patriotic national birthday song. The lyrics book includes over a dozen activity sheets. A complement of ten instrumental tracks allows students to become "performers"; boosting literacy skills and making "performances" a lot of fun.
IN ENGLISH

Bilingual Songs, vol. 1 and 2

The perfect way to have fun while acquiring a second language. Volume 1 teaches the basic alphabet, counting to 10, days of the week, months of the year, colors, food, animals, parts of the body, clothing and family members. Volume 2 teaches counting to 30, counting by 10s to 100, shapes and sizes, emotions, places in the community and the countryside, measurement and opposites. IN ENGLISH - SPANISH and ENGLISH - FRENCH

Please visit our web site, a great meeting place
for kids, teachers and parents on the Internet.
www.SongsThatTeach.com

For help in finding a retailer near you contact
Sara Jordan Publishing 1-800-567-7733